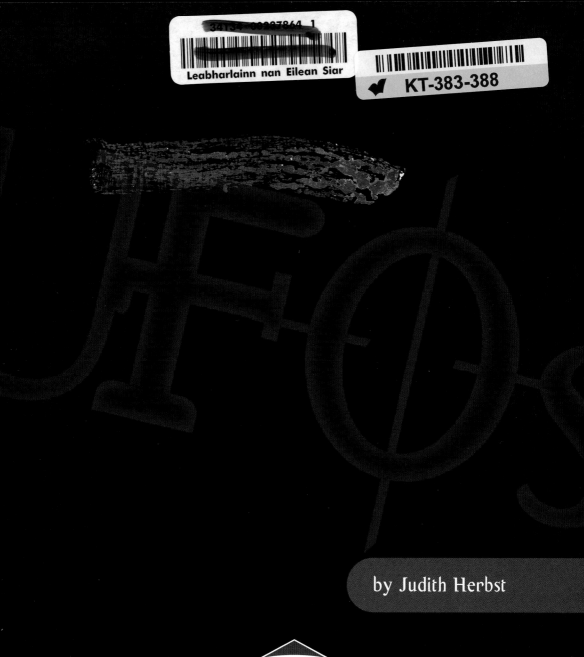

UFOs

by Judith Herbst

Lerner Books • London • New York • Minneapolis

First published in the United Kingdom in 2009 by
Lerner Books,
Dalton House,
60 Windsor Avenue,
London SW19 2RR

Website address: www.lernerbooks.co.uk

This edition was updated and edited for UK publication by Discovery Books Ltd.,
First Floor, 2 College Street, Ludlow, Shropshire SY8 1AN

British Library Cataloguing in Publication Data

Herbst, Judith
  UFOs. - 2nd ed. - (The unexplained)
  1. Unidentified flying objects - Juvenile literature
  I. Title
  001.9'42

ISBN-13: 978 0 7613 4312 7

Printed in Singapore

Table of Contents

Something

is seen,

but one doesn't

know what.

– Carl Jung

MARS ATTACKS

We have been dreaming about Mars for a long, long time. We have imagined crystal cities rising out of the red Martian sand. We have heard water rushing through the dry river beds. We have seen the Martian canals. A Martian breeze has touched our faces. In our hearts we always knew that we would meet them one day. They would come to our planet. The Martians.

It began in the 1700s, when astronomers turned their telescopes towards Mars and saw great wonders. There were two icy polar caps, just like on Earth. There were seasonal colour changes,

Astronomer William Herschel constructed this large reflecting telescope to observe the night sky. A complex of scaffolding supports the weight of the telescope.

as if winter were giving way to a blooming spring. There were bright, white patches. 'Clouds', whispered the English astronomer William Herschel. 'Those must be clouds.' Where there were clouds, there would be water. So by the 1800s, everyone simply assumed this planet, that was so much like Earth, would also have life.

Night after night, the astronomers struggled to sketch the face of Mars. However, the atmosphere often trembled and Martian dust storms blocked their view. A full moon rose and washed away the tiny planet in a blaze of light. Tantalized more than ever, the astronomers carried on. Close-up photographs of the Martian surface were still one hundred years into the future. So with sharp pencils the astronomers copied the faint lines they saw, each working alone in the starry night.

In 1840 two German astronomers published the first global map of Mars. However, they had no idea what they were looking at. Mars didn't really have any familiar features. There were no mountains or lakes or deep canyons – only white patches and dark, shadowy smears. The two astronomers gave all of the features names anyway. They called the dark areas oceans and seas. The lighter areas became continents.

It so happened that in Italy, an astronomer named Pietro Secchi had managed to make out some faint streaks on the planet's surface. Secchi didn't know what he was looking at either. So he decided to follow the custom and call the lines he saw *canali*. Of course, Secchi was speaking Italian and, in Italian, the word *canali* is not what it sounds like in

WHAT DID YOU BRING ME?

NASA plans to search for signs of Martian life include the Sample Return Lander, scheduled to leave Earth in October 2011. The most sophisticated space robot ever, the Lander will spend four months on the Red Planet, gathering souvenirs. In December 2012 it will launch itself, returning home with its samples nine months later. If any Martian life wants to stow away, that would be just lovely.

At one time, astronomers were convinced that the light and dark areas they saw on Mars were continents and oceans. This map of Mars from the 1800s shows the names scientists gave to areas of land and water, such as Herschel Continent and Dawes Ocean.

English. Canali are channels, or naturally forming stream beds. The English-speaking astronomers must not have had their Italian/English dictionaries handy because what they heard was 'canals', which are very different. Canals are artificial waterways. They are something that people build. So if Mars had canals, then it must also have . . . Martians? Oh, my!

Astronomers everywhere raced to their telescopes, anxious to see the canals for themselves. In America, William Pickering even added 'oases' to the scenes, which he said he saw where sections of the canals were joined to each other. At the Lick Observatory in California, USA, Edward Barnard just shrugged. Barnard was known to be a whizz at the telescope. He had sharp eyes and a lot of patience. However, try as he did, Barnard could not make out one single canal. Lines? Yes, there were plenty of lines, but lines were not waterways. A sceptical Barnard remained unconvinced.

The air, however, was crackling with Martian mania. Plans were even under way to try to signal the Martians. Nobody was more fever-ish with excitement than the American astronomer Percival Lowell. Lowell was so in love with

Percival Lowell (1855-1916) devoted much of his life to observing Mars. He built an observatory in Flagstaff, Arizona, USA, to aid him in his search for life on Mars.

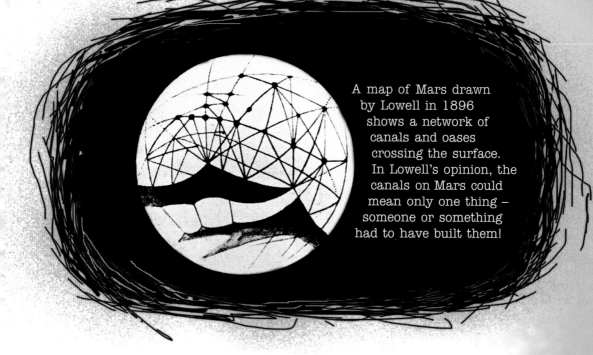

A map of Mars drawn by Lowell in 1896 shows a network of canals and oases crossing the surface. In Lowell's opinion, the canals on Mars could mean only one thing – someone or something had to have built them!

Mars that he had dipped into the family fortune and built himself an entire observatory just so he could study the planet. When he heard that canali had been discovered, he almost fell off his chair. (Obviously he didn't have an Italian/English dictionary either.) He went out into the icy night, prepared to freeze if necessary, for a good look. This would have been fine had Lowell kept his imagination in check. However, the thing got the better of him and Lowell began to fantasize.

Mars, he said, was dying. The water that had once flowed so freely was drying up. The planet was becoming a desert, whose red sands would blow and shift as the Martian winds howled across space. Alas, the polar caps were all that remained. So those brave little aliens had built a great system of canals to bring the water down from the poles to nourish the planet's thirsty inhabitants.

'Henderson', he called, 'you saw that shooting star last night?'

'Well?' said Henderson.

'It's out on Horsell Common now.'

'Good Lord!' said Henderson. 'Fallen meteorite! That's good.'

'But it's something more than a meteorite. It's a cylinder – an artificial cylinder, man! And there's something inside!'

– H G Wells,
The War of the Worlds

Lowell was so moved by his own sad story, he wrote a number of books describing the Martian woes. All the books were fiction, of course, but Lowell didn't think about that and neither did his readers. His fantasies sold quickly to a public that had come to believe in Martians. The Martians turned ugly in 1898, when English author H G Wells published his science fiction story, *The War of the Worlds.*

Wells's Martians were more insect-like than human and they were bent on destruction. They arrived in grey metallic cylinders with a plan to colonize Earth. Armed with death rays, the

A film still from the 1953 film based on H G Wells' *The War of the Worlds.* More than fifty years after the book was published in 1898, it still captured people's imaginations.

One of the earliest known photographs of an unexplained flying object (UFO) was taken on 27 July 1907, over Drobak, Norway. The UFO hovers in the sky above two sailing ships.

Martians blasted everything in sight and seemed to have the upper hand – or rather, tentacle. However, their alien chemistry was no match for Earth's bacteria, which eventually killed them off.

The War of the Worlds was wildly popular and when the century turned, Wells would see his story become even more spectacular.

≫ Halloween Hysterics

Sightings of UFOs, or unexplained flying objects, started quite some time ago. As early as 1907 sightings were being reported in Drobak, Norway and soon UFOs were being seen in every continent. This quietly fueled the Martian madness. Then, on the evening of 30 October 1938, Orson Welles caused an invasion scare that people still talk about to this day.

It was a Sunday, and the night before Halloween. Thousands of people had their radios tuned to the Columbia Broadcasting System's *Mercury Theatre on the Air* presentation. Orson Welles, the show's director, had planned a special scary treat for his listeners. At 8.00 pm sharp, the *Mercury Theatre* theme music rose and fell and Welles addressed the audience in a serious tone.

'We know now', he said, 'that in the early years of the Twentieth Century this world was being watched closely by intelligences greater than man's. . . . ' Listeners were riveted.

Welles set the stage. We were being studied, he said. As humans went about their business, somewhere *out there* plans were being made.

The programme cut to an announcer giving the weather report. Next came a supposedly live broadcast of dance music from the Meridian Room in the Park Plaza Hotel. Then Welles broke in. 'Ladies and gentlemen, we interrupt our programme of dance music to bring you a special bulletin from the Intercontinental Radio News.'

And so it began. Orson Welles had taken H G Wells's classic story *The War of the Worlds* and turned it into a fake news broadcast. The Martians, it seemed, had landed in New Jersey, not far from the city of New York, USA, and were blasting everything in sight with their ray guns. Earth was in big trouble. The audience heard it all as it was happening. That's what they thought, anyway, and they really panicked.

As the actors in the studio calmly read their lines, screaming people were filling the streets. Police stations were swamped with telephone calls. Roads were jammed. People prayed in Virginia and university students fainted in North Carolina. In San Francisco, volunteers lined up to fight the Martian invaders and in Pittsburgh, one woman was actually about to take poison when her husband came home, stopping her just in time.

Wild? It was very wild. Welles later admitted that he was shocked by the reaction. However, the listeners had been primed. Even before Secchi's canali announcement, respected astronomers had talked about life on Mars. UFOs were being seen. Hollywood was making films about rubbery space monsters and trips to the moon. Even the US government was beginning to wonder. The public simply became caught up in the madness, and it would only get crazier.

CHAPTER 2
AND SO IT BEGINS. . . .

Kenneth Arnold was not seeking publicity, but he got it. Big time. At about 3.00 pm on a June afternoon in 1947, Arnold spotted something a little strange through the window of his plane. He was heading south-east over the Cascade Mountains, on his way to Yakima, Washington, USA. Suddenly he saw. . . . Actually, he wasn't really sure what he saw. Nine objects, he said, flying at a fantastic speed. They were, perhaps, 3,000 metres up in the sky. Arnold watched with mounting curiosity as the objects dipped in and out of formation. Hmmm. Strange.

Arnold landed in Yakima, casually mentioned the event to a few people and took off again. When he arrived at Pendleton in Oregon, the journalists were waiting.

'Mr. Arnold! Mr. Arnold! What did you see up there?'

Arnold was somewhat puzzled. He had decided that the crescent-shaped objects had been secret army aircraft. After all, what else could they be? He patiently described his sighting to the press. He even drew a picture for them. 'They moved', he said, 'like a saucer skipping across the water'.

Kenneth Arnold (shown here with camera and on facing page with UFO drawing) reported seeing strange objects flying through the sky during a flight over the Cascade Mountains.

'A saucer!' shouted the press. 'You mean a *flying saucer?*'

'No', said Arnold. 'They were crescents. Look, here, just like in my drawing. . . . '

But the journalists paid no attention and that's how the term *flying saucer* was born.

» The Government Gets into the UFO Business

We still don't know what Kenneth Arnold saw in the clear skies that day. Some have said it was a flock of birds. Others believe it was just aeroplanes. Still others think Arnold had been fooled by some kind of optical illusion. But, whatever they were those nine bright objects caught the attention of the US government.

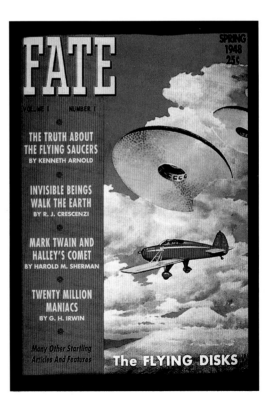

One year after Arnold's sighting, *Fate* magazine published this cover illustration of Arnold's encounter with what many people believe to have been flying saucers.

MR SMITH AND MR JONES

Part legend and part something else, the so-called Men in Black have been popping up since the 1950s. It is said that those who get too close to the 'truth' about flying saucers are apt to be visited by two or three men in black suits, white shirts, black ties and black trilby hats. Men in Black are mysterious, move like robots and warn witnesses to keep their mouths shut – or else!

Actually, the government had been troubled by reports of unidentified flying objects even before the Arnold sighting. If something's sneaking around up there and it's not ours, the government said, we want to know about it! So in 1948 they organized Project Sign.

Project Sign's mission was fairly straightforwards: find out what all those unidentified flying objects are and write a report. After a year of study, the investigators knew about as much as they did on the day they began – nothing. All they had managed to do was group the UFOs into four categories. These things were either flying discs, cigar-shaped bodies, spheres or balls of light that could climb, change direction and reach very high speeds.

Well, that's all very interesting, but what *were* they?

The authors of Project Sign had to admit they didn't know. It seems, they said, that whoever is building these aircraft is technically way ahead of the US. Perhaps it's the Soviet Union, they suggested, but they didn't

Astronomer Clyde Tombaugh, who discovered the planet Pluto, reported seeing pale yellow lights moving across the sky above Las Cruces, New Mexico, USA, on 20 August 1949. Tombaugh couldn't explain his sighting. This picture is an artist's impression of the event.

think that was possible.

All right, then. Who?

The UFOs, the authors of Project Sign said, might be 'aerial visitors from another planet'.

This kind of suggestion scared everyone, so that was the end of Project Sign. It was not, however, the end of the sightings, which were numbering in the hundreds. Like a mosquito that keeps buzzing around your head, UFOs continued to appear. So in 1949, the US government launched Project Grudge.

Okay, said the members of Project Grudge a year later. We studied the situation and we have to tell you that these UFOs are a whole lot of nonsense. They are not super advanced flying machines. There are no aliens inside them and they did not come from another planet. In fact, many of the sightings are mistakes. You know, people see the planet Venus. It's very bright and they think it's a UFO. Of course, a lot of the reports are hoaxes. People are fibbing, making up stories. The rest are just hallucinations. Thank you very much. This concludes our report.

It's hard to know if the government was relieved. Probably not, because the UFOs didn't look like they had any intention of going away. If anything, they became even more maddening. 'So we don't exist, do we?' they seemed to be saying. 'Well, can you see this?!' In September 1951, a UFO showed up on army radar, of all places. The object was spotted on radar at Fort Monmouth, New Jersey. It was moving so fast, the air traffic controller couldn't even track it. In a 48-hour period, a total of four UFOs were picked up on the radar. And when the pilot of a T-33 jet reported seeing an unidentified object some 10 to 15 m in diameter, everybody agreed that this sort of thing could not be allowed

This photograph was taken in July 1952 in the sky over New York City, USA. Some UFO sightings have proven to be hoaxes and some can be explained by natural phenomena. There are other sightings that remain mysteries.

AND SO IT BEGINS....

The staff of Project Blue Book stands behind Major Hector Quintanilla Jr. Of a total of 12,618 sightings reported to Project Blue Book between 1947 and 1969, 701 remain unidentified.

to continue. So the government called back Project Grudge, changed its name to Project Blue Book and demanded that it identify the UFOs.

>> Does Radar Lie?

For whatever reason, things became very lively in the summer of 1952. Just before midnight on 19 July eight UFOs appeared over the centre of the US government in Washington – known as the Capitol. Witnesses – and there were plenty of them – said the objects zipped this way and that, changing direction with amazing speed. Since it was dark, no one actually saw any discss – only lights. However, there must have been something solid in the sky, because it all showed up very clearly on radar.

Harry Barnes was the area's chief air traffic controller at the time. He immediately gave the order to send a squadron of jets to intercept the . . . uh . . . lights. The jets had to come from a base far away in Wilmington, Delaware and – you guessed it – by the time the jets arrived, the lights were gone. So the jets started heading back to their base, but as soon as they left Washington, the lights were back. Playing a game of hide and seek, perhaps?

EARTH VERSUS THE FLYING SAUCERS

The Washington UFO flap was a dream come true for Hollywood. In 1956 special effects master Ray Harryhausen worked his way into cinemas with Earth versus the Flying Saucers. In the film, the aliens were eventually shot out of the sky by an anti-flying-saucer death ray, which saved the day but totally wrecked Washington. The smouldering flying saucer sticking out of a popular Washington monument was a nice touch.

The government didn't think any of this was funny and it became even less funny when the UFOs showed up again one week later. From 9.00 pm until 2.00 am, radar tracked as many as 12 UFOs, all silently dancing over the Capitol. So again jets were scrambled, and again the UFOs disappeared just in time. Back went the jets to base. Back came the UFOs.

At 3.00 am, another squadron of jets was sent to Washington, but this time the UFOs hung around and pilot Lieutenant William Patterson spotted them. 'I can see the lights', he reported. 'They're bluish-white and tremendous. Tremendous!'

The air traffic controllers back on the ground could hardly

AND SO IT BEGINS . . .

21

believe what they were hearing.

'They're just ahead of me,' said Patterson, 'in a kind of cluster. I'm approaching.'

Then, 'They've formed a ring around me.' Patterson's voice was shaking. 'What should I do?'

The controllers were speechless. But, if they had a good idea up their sleeves, Patterson would never hear about it. Seconds later, the UFO circle broke up and Patterson found himself alone in the sky.

The Washington sightings had so many eyewitnesses that there was no way government officials could ignore what had happened. They had to say something. So on 29 July they held a press conference. They announced that the unknown targets observed over Washington were the result of a temperature inversion.

Of course, that was silly and the government knew it. A temperature inversion is just a layer of air in which the temperature increases rather than decreases with height. But they must have thought it was better to sound silly than ignorant.

The CIA put together a panel to investigate the situation. Perhaps a group of scientists could work it all out. However, the scientists weren't really interested in UFOs and they made rather fast work of it. UFOs are known objects, they said. There's no threat to national security (even though the UFOs had entered restricted airspace when they flew over the Capitol). There aren't any aliens and we strongly recommend that future UFO reports be dismissed as nonsense. The public is getting too worked up.

This UFO was photographed by George J Stock in Passaic, New Jersey, USA, on 19 July 1952.

When Project Blue Book came to the same conclusions, the astronomer J Allen Hynek fired off a letter to the Office of the Secretary of the US Air Force. Hynek was troubled. I think you have to turn this problem over to a panel of civilian scientists, he said. Somebody has to review the findings of Project Blue Book.

They actually agreed to this, probably because they were tired of the whole UFO thing. So in 1966, the University of Colorado signed a contract with the air force to investigate UFO reports. Unfortunately, the Colorado Project, as it was called, got nowhere. In fact, we're still bumbling around in the dark. Over the years, there have been thousands of sightings. Most can be explained, but some can't. The UFOs' radar tracks are real. The photos people take of them are real. The marks they leave behind are real. Something is definitely seen. We just don't know what it is.

CHAPTER 3
THE ROSWELL INCIDENT

Without a doubt, the Roswell Incident is the most famous UFO case of all time. It occurred in 1947, one week after Kenneth Arnold's sighting. Just because it's famous doesn't mean it tells the true story of a crashed UFO. The only thing we know for sure is that something fell on Mac Brazel's ranch in Roswell, New Mexico, USA, and smashed apart. The government said it was a weather balloon. Others insist it was a flying saucer carrying five aliens. Will we ever find out what it really was?

The mythology around this incident is thick. It has been accumulating for more than 50 years. Almost everyone involved in the incident has passed away and the site has been swept clean of any bits of evidence it may have had. So the legend continues to grow.

Astronomer Carl Sagan (*left*) believed that we would one day discover life in the universe, but he seriously doubted that flying saucers were evidence of it.

If anything, the Roswell Incident shows how badly we want to believe in aliens. It makes our hearts race faster and sends our imaginations on a roller coaster ride. As astronomer Carl Sagan once said, 'Extraordinary claims demand extraordinary proof'. And this story makes some very extraordinary claims. This is what happened.

It is 1 July 1947. Strange blips start showing up on three different army radar screens. They move very fast and change direction suddenly. Nobody has the slightest idea what they are.

The following evening, a fierce thunderstorm rips through the skies over Roswell, New Mexico. Dan Wilmot goes out onto his patio after dinner to watch the lightning show. The storm is fantastic. Between lightning flashes, Dan and his wife see something very bright streak across the sky. It falls towards the north-east and drops behind the horizon. A milkman called Steve Robinson sees the same object. He describes it as bright, oval and solid.

On 3 July Mac Brazel finds some kind of wreckage strewn over a large area of his ranch. He later told people that some of it was very shiny, like metal, but it was also very light. When he

Area 51

UFO buffs dream of making a pilgrimage to Area 51 in Nevada – not that they would ever be allowed in. Area 51 is a top secret army test site, where the so-called X-planes (short for 'experimental planes') are assembled and flown. People living nearby report seeing strange lights zipping back and forth across the sky late at night, fuelling the rumour that engineers were able to build a working model of the Roswell saucer.

Seven days after the crash in Roswell, New Mexico, USA, the *Roswell Daily Record* ran a headline announcing that no details of the captured flying disc had been revealed.

tried crumpling it up, it just unfolded. It didn't dent when he pounded it with a sledgehammer. He also claimed to have seen strange symbols on several pieces of the debris.

Brazel called the army air base at Roswell to report the crash. Major Jesse Marcel immediately showed up with a team and began to clear away the wreckage. Then a very curious thing happened. The army issued a press release stating that it had captured a flying saucer.

Now, let's stop right here. The government had been doing its best to play down the whole UFO thing. Flying saucers? Ridiculous! You saw clouds. You saw the lights on a blimp. You were dreaming. You were hallucinating. You were lying.

So why would the army tell the newspapers that a flying saucer had crashed in New Mexico? It makes no sense. But let's go on.

Major Marcel's recovery team scooped up all of the debris and took it back to the base. It was then flown to Wright-Patterson Air Force Base in Ohio. Another press release was issued. The army had apparently changed its mind. It wasn't a flying saucer that crashed. It was a weather balloon. A weather balloon? Is that possible? Yes.

In the summer of 1947, the navy had begun launching enormous weather balloons under the name Operation Skyhook. The Skyhook balloons were teardrop shaped and made of a very thin plastic film. They carried an instrument pack high into the stratosphere to measure, among other things, cosmic rays.

The balloons had been developed in the General Mills research labs in Minneapolis, so everybody there knew all about them. However, most people didn't. Even the folks in Minneapolis mistook the Skyhooks for UFOs. The balloons drifted so high up, you couldn't make out their

The army claimed the Roswell debris was really the wreckage of a weather balloon. This photograph shows a Skyhook balloon.

shape. Because they reflected sunlight, they looked like dancing spots of light. That made them the perfect UFO, except, of course, they weren't.

If you had seen one of these balloons lying on the ground, you'd almost certainly know what it was, but there was a terrible storm the night before the Roswell crash. All that wild weather could have easily brought down one of the balloons. The instrument pack would have been smashed to smithereens, and the balloon wouldn't have fared any better. So out goes Mac Brazel the next day and sees the wreckage. It all looks unfamiliar to him. It is, in fact, very high tech. Brazel's a farmer, remember, not a scientist. He doesn't recognize the material. He sees symbols that he can't identify, but would you recognize these symbols?

They certainly look like a strange language, but they're actually weather symbols. In fact, these symbols might very well have been on the Skyhook instrument packs. Would Brazel have known what they were? Did you know what they were?

≫ All This and Aliens Too.

There's more to this story, though. Over the years, dozens of people have been interviewed about the Roswell case and some have made some shocking claims. Here's a sample:

· They saw parts of the crashed saucer.
· They saw five dead aliens.

ALIEN FLIGHT SCHOOL

Arguably, the most bizarre UFO story ever told comes from the scientist Robert Lazar. Lazar claims that in 1987 he was approached by naval intelligence and asked to work on a top secret project at Groom Lake, the site of Area 51. Lazar says he spent about one year at a facility called S-4, trying to reconstruct one of several alien saucers the government had got its hands on.

Lazar, whose speciality is systems engineering, was told that UFOs use gravity amplification – whatever that is – to move around and fly, and that they are partly fueled by Element 115, a very heavy, radioactive metal that does not exist on Earth.

According to Lazar, the spacecraft he worked on was 12 m in diameter and had three levels. The middle level had seats for a crew of three aliens and the lowest level housed the gravity amplifiers. Lazar was not allowed to see the uppermost level.

Lazar claims that this particular model was briefly test-flown. It didn't get more than a few metres above the ground, but its underside did give off a blue glow.

· One of the aliens was still alive at the scene but later died.
· They watched the autopsy of the aliens.
· The saucer remains in a top secret location.

What are we to make of all this? Well, first we should remember what Carl Sagan said. Extraordinary claims demand extraordinary proof. So where's the proof?

A number of years ago, an American TV network aired a film that was supposed to show the autopsy of one of the Roswell aliens.

However, you would have to be awfully gullible to be taken in by this. The 'autopsy' looked like something a group of high school students would do for a prank. It was completely unprofessional and the technique was all wrong. The 'alien' was even worse. The film wasn't very clear either and there were, of course, no close-ups. A close-up would have shown the alien for what it most likely was – a piece of rubber. You also have to ask yourself why the film of a real alien autopsy wasn't classified as top secret. When the government wants to hide something, it does a very good job.

Okay. So maybe the autopsy was faked, but what about the people who claimed to have seen dead aliens? Without proof, all we have is their word – if it really is their word.

If you've ever played 'Chinese whispers', you know how a message can change when it is passed from person to person. The Roswell Incident is over 50 years old. How many people have repeated the story? How many writers have used what others wrote as their source of information? Did all these people check their facts? Did these so-called eye-witnesses really exist in the first place, or are they just part of the mythology? If somebody is asking you to believe in aliens, the proof has to be good.

Until his death, Major Marcel insisted he had never seen anything like the Roswell wreckage. However, Marcel was a staff intelligence officer. He had nothing to do with Operation Skyhook. So a downed balloon would have been just as unfamiliar to him as it was to Mac Brazel. There's also another possibility. The crashed object could have been an experimental aircraft.

Roswell, New Mexico, is not far from the White Sands Missile Range. White Sands is not open to the public. Guess why. This is where the government tests its most secret missile and aircraft designs. Once the

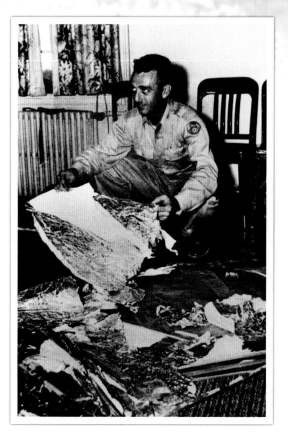

Major Jesse Marcel poses with the remains of a tattered weather balloon.

aircraft are built, they have to be taken out and test-flown. So imagine a craft that's still experimental. All the quirks are not sorted out yet. On a test flight, the pilot gets into trouble. The plane crashes during a severe thunderstorm and the debris scatters over a large area. Mac Brazel finds it. 'Wow!' he thinks. 'What on earth is *this*?'

The government now has a problem. Should they tell the public about this top secret aircraft? No! So they announce that the army has captured a UFO. Then a couple of days later, they decide the UFO story might get out of hand – which it did. So they change it. The wreckage becomes a weather balloon. It's not nearly as exciting as a crashed flying saucer packed with little aliens, but it's not as fantastic either.

In the world of UFOs, there are seekers of truth and dreamers of dreams. The truth is hard to unearth. So step carefully and remember what Carl Sagan said. If and when the aliens arrive, chances are, we'll know it.

C H A P T E R   4

A UFO SAMPLER

32

Not everyone who reports a UFO actually sees a UFO. The sky is filled with many things that people simply don't recognize. Unusual cloud formations, meteorites, orbiting satellites, Venus. However, there are times when a sighting cannot be so easily explained. Here are some of the cases that have truly baffled the investigators. Whatever these people saw remains a mystery.

This UFO photograph *(facing page)* was taken in 1969, in Alabama, USA.

>> Case 1

Gujan-Mestras, France, 19 June 1978

It is 1.30 am. Monsieur Bachère is driving west towards Bordeaux. As he approaches the town of La Réole, he sees a 'large orange ball, very bright', hovering about 300 m up in the night sky. Suddenly it disappears, only to reappear a minute later. Monsieur Bachère and his wife exchange looks and continue on their way.

In Gujan-Mestras, Monsieur Varisse is in his shop, baking fresh loaves of crusty bread for the morning. Perhaps he is whistling. Suddenly there is a knock at the door. Monsieur Varisse looks up. 'Eh? Someone is here? At this hour?' He wipes his floury hands on his apron and crosses the room to see who it is.

Two teenagers are on the steps, shaking, terrified. They had pulled off the road, they tell him, to see if they could mend the broken indicator in their car. Suddenly, all the street lights went out and they heard a powerful rumble. It sounded like an earthquake. They looked up and saw something red and oval about 300 m high, heading straight for them.

Monsieur Varisse laughs. They are joking, of course. It is a teenage prank. He asks their names.

'Frank Pavia', says the one who looks a bit older.

The other boy is very upset. His eyes are red and moist.

33

'Jean-Marc', he stammers. 'Jean-Marc Guitard.'

This oval, they continue, was surrounded with white flames. Jean-Marc found it hard to breathe. Then he fainted. That's when the object changed direction and flew away. The boys are trembling.

Monsieur Varisse laughs again.

When the boys' story reached the offices of GEPAN, the French centre for UFO studies, nobody laughed. Others in the area had reported strange happenings that night. GEPAN decided to investigate.

Three scientists visited the site the following day. They interviewed the witnesses and took them back to the place where they had seen the object. The witnesses described the object's colour and movements and estimated its height above the ground. Soon additional witnesses started coming forwards. A student who lived in Gujan-Mestras reported seeing orange flashes above the trees just as the street lights went out. That had been about 12.30 pm, he said. He had also heard a low rumble. The witnesses agreed on the colour of the object, as well as its size. Certainly the most interesting aspect was the UFO's power output, which had been enough to trip the photoelectric cells in the street lights. Conclusion: a very bright disc-shaped object with a diameter of about 5 m had flown low over Gujan-Mestras, France, identity unknown.

>> Case 2

Trans-en-Provence, France, 8 January 1981

It is about 5.00 pm. Monsieur Nicolai is outside, building a concrete water pump behind his house. Suddenly, he hears 'a faint whistling'. He turns and sees 'a device in the air', just about level with the top of a large pine tree. The object begins to descend. The whistling sound continues. Monsieur Nicolai moves closer. He would later recall that the object was not spinning, nor did he see any flames coming from it.

Monsieur Nicolai is about 25 m away when he sees the device touch down. It remains on the ground for perhaps a second or two and then rises again. As it moves off, Monsieur Nicolai notices four openings on the underside of the object. He does not see any flames or smoke. The object heads north-east at a very high rate of speed and in moments it is gone. A little while later, Monsieur Nicolai walks to the spot where the object landed and finds a circle about 2 m in diameter. He also sees what looks like scratched areas here and there around the circle. The following morning, his wife and neighbour examine the circle. They urge Monsieur Nicolai to call the police.

About five weeks later, a team from GEPAN arrived to investigate the sighting. Soil and plant samples were taken and Monsieur Nicolai was questioned several times. He said that the object was shaped like 'two saucers, one inverted on top of the other', ringed by a thick ridge. He described it as being the colour of lead. Underneath were four circles.

There was a two-and-a-half-metre tall retaining wall on the property, which helped Monsieur Nicolai estimate the size of the object. He worked out that the diameter was about 2.5 m and the height, no bigger than 2 m.

Soil samples from the landing site were sent away for analysis. Tests determined that the soil had been subjected to pressure and heat. Large, black particles found in the soil appeared to be combustion residue.

GEPAN was unable to draw any conclusions based on their investigations. The event remains unidentified.

>> Case 3

Irvine, California, USA, 3 August 1965

It is just past noon. Rex Heflin, a motorway maintenance engineer, pulls off the road to photograph a railroad crossing sign. Branches have grown over the sign, blocking it from view. It is Heflin's job to report this sort of thing.

Heflin reaches for the camera he always carries. He is just about to photograph the sign when he catches a flash of something out of the corner of his eye. Heflin is parked near the crossroads of Myford Road and Walnut Avenue, eight kilometres (five miles) from El Toro Marine Base.

ROADSIDE UFOS

Travel America and you'll see how much they love flying saucers. Not far from Austin, Texas, the Association for the Understanding of Man has set up an array of lights to help guide UFOs to a safe landing. There's another landing site in Pennsylvania. In Tennessee, Curtis King lives in a flying saucer-shaped house and Al Thomas of Russellville, Arkansas, has a home made flying saucer in a hangar behind his garage.

As the object approaches, Heflin can see that it is a silvery-coloured craft of some sort. He assumes it's from the marine base. Something experimental, perhaps. As the craft crosses Myford Road, Heflin takes a picture of it through the van's windscreen. The craft continues eastwards, tilting just enough to show a dark underside. That's when Heflin sees the beam of green-white light. It is coming from the very centre of the craft, rotating clockwise, sweeping out a complete circle every two seconds. Heflin takes a second picture, this time through the passenger window.

At this point, the craft seems to wobble a little, as if it is losing stability. It begins to turn and Heflin takes a third picture. The craft is still moving away. Heflin gets a fourth and final picture as the object starts to climb, leaving what Heflin describes as a 'smoke-like vapour'. Moments later, it shoots off and is swallowed up by the clouds. Heflin still thinks he has seen an experimental aircraft.

Here's where the story gets really interesting.

This series of photographs taken by Heflin through his van window shows some sort of aircraft flying past. The bottom photograph shows the 'smoke-like vapour' Heflin claims to have seen.

The publisher of the *Santa Ana Register* learned about Heflin's photos and printed the story. As a result, intelligence officers showed up at Heflin's house. Then the US air force got involved. Heflin was interviewed for more than three hours. Eventually, the sighting was labelled as a hoax, even though the investigating officer's report stated that Heflin '*is not* attempting to perpetrate a hoax'.

Then . . . on 22 September two men knocked on Heflin's door. They claimed to be from the North American Aerospace Defense Command (NORAD). They asked to borrow three of the four photographs. Heflin gave them the pictures and that's the last he saw of the men. Their identity was never discovered. The object Heflin photographed remains unidentified.

>> Case 4

Mansfield, Ohio, 18 October 1973

This is known as the Coyne Helicopter Case and it is about as intriguing as a UFO sighting can ever be. The witnesses were the four-man crew of an army reserve helicopter.

It is close to 11.00 pm, Sergeants John Healey and Robert Yanacsek, Lieutenant Arrigo Jezzi and Captain Lawrence Coyne are on their way back to base in Cleveland, USA. They are flying at an altitude of 750 m. Their airspeed is roughly 165 kph (102 mph). Suddenly Healey, who is in the left rear seat, spots a red light off to the west. It is heading south.

Just after 11.00 pm Yanacsek, in the right rear seat, sees a single red light on the eastern horizon. The light seems to be keeping pace with the helicopter. Yanacsek alerts Coyne, who tells him to 'keep an eye on it'. Thirty seconds later, the light begins closing in on the helicopter. Jezzi has been at the controls, but at this point Coyne takes over. He begins a powered descent, dropping at a speed of 150 m per minute. He contacts the Mansfield control tower and asks about air traffic in the area. Before Mansfield can respond, all contact is lost.

Meanwhile, the red light continues to advance. It seems, in fact, to be heading straight for the helicopter.

'That thing must be doing over 1,000 kilometres per hour!'

Coyne speeds up the helicopter's descent, but the light keeps coming. Then it slows and hangs there in front of the helicopter. Now Coyne, Healey and Yanacsek can see that it is a grey, metallic, object, shaped like a cigar. It is absolutely enormous. A green beam spills from the underside. Rooted to their seats and speechless, the men watch as the beam sweeps across the windscreen, bathing the interior in green light. There is no noise and no turbulence. Coyne's hand is still on the altitude control, but instead of descending, the helicopter is climbing. It is now at 1,050 m and moving higher at a rate of 300 m per minute. The object hovers for a few more seconds, then suddenly shoots away.

Five ground witnesses confirmed the sighting. From their car, one adult and four children saw both the helicopter and the object. 'It was big' said the oldest boy. 'It lit up everything.' Despite a thorough investigation, the object encountered by the helicopter crew remains a mystery.

An artist's impression of the UFO Captain Lawrence Coyne and his crew saw while flying.

CHAPTER 5

SOMETHING IS SEEN . . . bUT WHAT IS IT?

We like to think we are very clever. We have peered into the heart of the atom. We have gazed outwards through space. We can almost describe what conditions were like shortly after the big bang, the explosion that gave birth to the universe. However, there are still many things that we don't understand or even know about. UFOs are in this category.

Scientists with open minds are finding it harder and harder to deny the existence of UFOs. These things – whatever they are – leave traces. They scorch the ground. They crush the grass. They trip the photoelectric cells in street lights. They show up on radar. Then, they are gone, like a puff of smoke or a ghost. Like the images in a dream.

Lenticular (lens-shaped) clouds *(below and facing page)*
are sometimes mistaken for UFOs.

Sometimes they seem to be under intelligent control. However, if
they are alien spacecraft, how can they just disappear? Where do
they come from? Where do they go? Do they just pop into another
universe? Is there another universe?

There really aren't any theories – only suggestions. Here they are.

UFOs are spaceships from another planet. It's possible, of course,
but it means accepting the following:

- Other planets that are favourable to life exist somewhere in the
  universe. (There is no proof of this yet.)
- The beings have somehow worked out where we are. (Earth
  circles a medium-sized star towards the edge of a galaxy filled
  with billions of stars. Basically, we're very hard to find.)

If It's Not A UFO, What Is It?

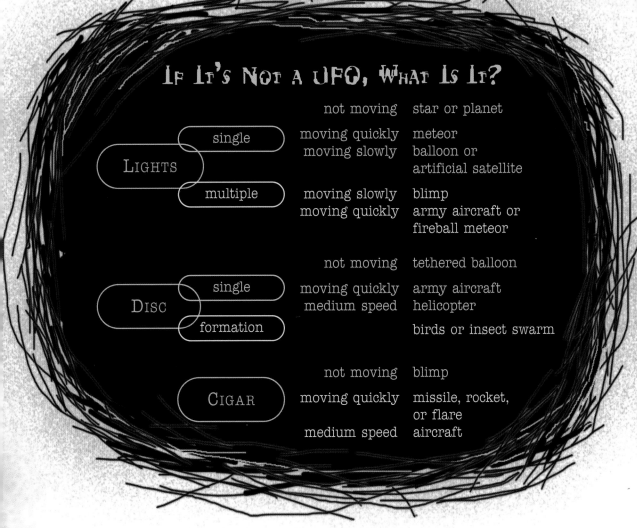

LIGHTS	single	not moving — star or planet
		moving quickly — meteor
		moving slowly — balloon or artificial satellite
	multiple	moving slowly — blimp
		moving quickly — army aircraft or fireball meteor
DISC	single	not moving — tethered balloon
		moving quickly — army aircraft
		medium speed — helicopter
	formation	birds or insect swarm
CIGAR		not moving — blimp
		moving quickly — missile, rocket, or flare
		medium speed — aircraft

- The ships are either remote controlled, or the aliens are very small. (Many UFOs seem to be no larger than the average bedroom. Those, of course, could be drone ships – ships without pilots.)
- The aliens are surveying us for some reason, or they just like scaring us.

That's an awful lot to swallow. Remember what Carl Sagan said.

44

UFOs are holograms. This is a very cool idea. A hologram, of course, is a three-dimensional image created by beams of light. So this would suggest that UFOs are essentially ghosts. The problem here, though, is that a hologram would not be able to crush grass or leave burn marks.

UFOs are warps in the fabric of space-time. This is so weird that if UFOs turn out to be space-time warps, we still won't know what they are.

UFOs are objects that exist alongside us but that we cannot normally perceive through our five senses. Wow! What an amazing idea! It's not as bizarre as it sounds.

Our five senses are good, but they don't pick up everything. Our eyes, for example, can see only a very narrow range of wavelengths. We can't see X-rays, ultraviolet rays, microwaves, infrared rays and lots more. Our sense of smell is nowhere near that of a shark's. Dogs can hear frequencies that are way beyond us. So what makes us think that we are getting the whole picture? There might be an awful lot of stuff going on around us that we don't know about. But perhaps, every so often, we catch a glimpse of it. Its an intriguing idea, to be sure.

That, alas, is where we must leave it. For a very long time, few scientists considered UFOs worthy of study. They're beginning to change their minds, however. These things simply won't go away. The evidence – although sketchy – suggests that *something* is going on. So keep your eyes on the sky, because just when you least expect it, who knows? You may just catch that glimpse. . . .

>> Find Out More

Books

Evans, Chris. *Aliens and UFOs* Carlton Books Ltd., 2008.

Oxlade, Chris. *The Mystery of UFOs* (Can Science Solve) Heinemann Library, 2007.

Wells, H G. *The War of the Worlds* Penguin Classics, 2005.

Websites

The Royal Observatory
http://www.nmm.ac.uk/server/show/nav.3554
Part of the National Maritime Museum, the Royal Observatory website has lots of information about early and modern star gazing.

The Skeptiseum
www.skeptiseum.org
This virtual museum has images of artefacts and souvenirs related to topics such as UFOs and aliens, ghosts, ESP and legendary creatures like Bigfoot and the Loch Ness Monster. The website is hosted by CSICOP, the Committee for the Scientific Investigation of Claims of the Paranormal.

Films

War of the Worlds Live Universal Pictures Video, 2006.
Watch a live performance of Jeff Wayne's orchestral version of War of the Worlds.

ET – The Extra Terrestrial Universal, 1982. DVD.
In this family-friendly story an alien meets a boy named Eliot, who then helps his new friend 'ET' to 'phone home' and be reunited with his family .

>> About the Author

Born in Baltimore, Maryland, USA, Judith Herbst grew up in Queens, New York, where she learned to jump double skipping ropes with amazing skill. She has since lost that ability. A former English teacher, she ran away from school to become a writer. Her first book for children was *Sky Above and Worlds Beyond,* whose title, she admits, was much too long. She loves to write and would rather be published, she says, than be rich, which has turned out to be the case. Herbst spends her summers in Maine on a lake with her cats and laptop.

>> Photo Acknowledgements

Photographs and illustrations in this book are used with the permission of: © Christel Gerstenberg/CORBIS, p 6; Fortean Picture Library, pp 7, 9, 11, 12, 14, 15, 18, 19, 20, 26, 27, 31, 32, 38, 39 (all), 41, 42, 43; © Bettmann/CORBIS, p 8; Hollywood Book and Poster, p 10; Llewellyn Publications/Fortean Picture Library, p 16; August C Roberts/Fortean Picture Library, p 23; AP/Wide World Photos, p 25.
Maps and illustrations by Bill Hauser/Independent Picture Service, pp 4-5, 25, 33, 34, 35, 37, 40.
Cover image by Fortean Picture Library.